CORN!

A MY INCREDIBLE WORLD PICTURE BOOK

MY INCREDIBLE WORLD

Corn is a tall, green plant grown
in fields all around the world.

1

Corn, also known as **maize** in many countries, is a type of grain, just like wheat, rice, and oats.

It is one of the most important crops and has been cultivated for thousands of years!

The part of the corn plant we eat is called the **ear** or **cob**, and it's full of delicious **kernels**.

The average corn plant has up to 4 corn cobs, each with around 800 kernels!

The ear is actually part of the corn's flower, and the kernels are the seeds of the corn plant!

Kernels come in lots of colors
like yellow, white, blue,
red, and even black!

Corn is used to make many
foods, such as popcorn, tortillas,
cornbread, and corn chips.

Popcorn is a special type of corn kernel that expands and pops when heated!

Sweet corn is the kind of corn we eat, while **field corn** is used to feed animals.

Corn can also used to make
fuel, medicine, cosmetics,
glue, and even crayons!

Corn grows best in warm weather, and it loves lots of sunshine.

Farmers plant corn seeds in rows and take care of the plants as they grow.

Corn is generally planted in spring, and harvested in late summer and fall.

Some corn plants grow taller than people, reaching up to 8 feet (2.4 m)!

The long flowers at the top of a corn plant are called **tassels**, and they produce its pollen.

The stringy strands at the end of each cob are called **silks**, and there is one for each kernel!

17

In autumn, some people like
to decorate with corn and
corn stalks.

Exploring mazes made in corn fields, called **corn mazes**, is also a fun fall activity!

The United States is the largest producer of corn, growing about a third of all the world's corn!

Every year, about a billion metric tons are harvested — that's the weight of 250 million elephants!

Corn is incredible!

Made in United States
Troutdale, OR
10/23/2023